How To Grow A 5 Billion Dollar IRA: Strategies of the Elite Revealed

Harmony Weaver

Copyright © 2024 by Harmony Weaver All rights reserved. No part of this publication may be reproduced, distributed, or transmitted in any form or by any means, including photocopying, recording, or other electronic or mechanical methods, without the prior written permission of the publisher, except in the case of brief quotations embodied in critical reviews and certain other noncommercial uses permitted by copyright law.

Disclaimer... 7
Preface...8
Introduction: Unlocking the Secrets of Mega IRAs........... 11
Chapter 1: The Evolution of the IRA................................... 20
Chapter 2: The Peter Thiel Strategy.....................................31
Chapter 3: Achieving Mega IRA Status............................... 37
Chapter 4: Investing in Non-Publicly Traded Shares........ 44
Chapter 5: Building Wealth with Private Equity.................62
Chapter 6: The Policy Landscape: Senate Finance Committee Response.. 76
Chapter 7: Final Considerations and Cautionary Tales.... 82
Conclusion... 88

Disclaimer

The information provided in this book is for educational and informational purposes only. It is not intended as financial, investment, tax, or legal advice. Readers are advised to consult with qualified professionals, such as financial advisors, tax consultants, or attorneys, before making any financial decisions or implementing any strategies discussed in this book. The author and publisher disclaim any liability for any loss or damage resulting from reliance on the information provided herein. All investment involves risk, and past performance is not indicative of future results.

Preface

As a writer immersed in the worlds of spirituality, mysticism, and self-help, venturing into the arena of finance and retirement planning may seem like a departure from familiar territory. Yet, it is precisely this departure into the unknown that has led on a new exploration, one that examines the complexities of wealth accumulation, tax strategies, and the quest for financial security.

The genesis of this book, "How To Grow A 5 Billion Dollar IRA: Strategies of the Elite Revealed," traces back to a pivotal moment of curiosity sparked by an article I stumbled upon an article that shed light on the phenomenon of Mega IRAs and the extraordinary wealth amassed within them. Intrigued by the intersection of finance, tax policy, and societal implications, I became determined to unravel the intricacies of this intriguing topic.

In the pages that follow, I invite you to join me on a voyage through the labyrinthine corridors of retirement planning, investment strategies, and the policy landscape surrounding Mega IRAs. Drawing upon insights from financial experts, tax professionals, and policymakers, we will navigate the terrain of wealth accumulation, empowering ourselves with knowledge and guidance to make informed decisions about our financial futures.

While my previous works have explored the inner dimensions of the human experience, this book represents a departure into the external realm of material wealth and financial well-being. Yet, in essence, the quest for financial security is intricately intertwined with our spiritual journey of self-discovery, empowerment, and alignment with our highest aspirations.

May we cultivate a deeper understanding of the forces shaping our financial destinies and harness the wisdom gained to chart a course towards a future of abundance, prosperity, and fulfillment.

With gratitude,

Harmony Weaver

Introduction: Unlocking the Secrets of Mega IRAs

In the world of retirement savings, there exists a select group of individuals who have mastered the art of wealth accumulation with unparalleled precision and audacity. Their stories are the stuff of legend, whispered in hushed tones among the financial elite and scrutinized with fascination by the masses. At the center of this intrigue lies the Mega IRA. A seemingly ordinary retirement account transformed into a vehicle for amassing billions of dollars in tax-free wealth.

In "How To Grow A 5 Billion Dollar IRA: Strategies of the Elite Revealed," we take a deep dive into this clandestine world, peeling back the layers of secrecy to uncover the strategies, tactics, and loopholes exploited by the financial elite to achieve unimaginable levels of wealth within their retirement accounts. At the heart of our exploration is the enigmatic figure of Peter Thiel, whose Roth IRA success story serves as both a beacon of inspiration and a cautionary tale for aspiring wealth builders.

But before we delve into the intricacies of Mega IRAs and the strategies employed to build them, let us first set the stage by tracing the evolution of the Individual Retirement Account. Born out of a desire to provide American workers with a means to save for retirement, the IRA has undergone a remarkable transformation since its inception. From its humble beginnings as a modest tax-advantaged savings vehicle, the IRA has evolved into a powerful tool for wealth accumulation, offering individuals the opportunity to harness the power of compound growth and tax deferral to build a secure financial future.

The Roth IRA, in particular, has captured the imagination of investors with its promise of tax-free growth and withdrawals. Unlike its traditional counterpart, which offers tax deductions on contributions but taxes withdrawals as ordinary income, the Roth IRA flips the script by requiring contributions to be made with after-tax dollars in exchange for tax-free withdrawals in retirement. It is within this framework that the strategies of the financial elite truly come to life, as they leverage the unique advantages of the Roth IRA to achieve outsized returns and accumulate vast fortunes.

Enter Peter Thiel, a Silicon Valley titan and master of the Mega IRA. Thiel's journey from humble beginnings to billionaire status is a testament to the power of strategic investing and long-term vision. At the heart of Thiel's Roth IRA strategy is a simple yet profound insight: invest in high-growth companies through a tax-advantaged account. By seizing opportunities to acquire shares in promising startups at rock-bottom prices, Thiel was able to capitalize on the exponential growth potential of early-stage investments and multiply his initial capital many times over.

The eBay-PayPal saga stands as a prime example of Thiel's investment prowess. In 1999, Thiel made a modest investment of just $1,700 to acquire 1.7 million shares of PayPal at a par value of $0.001 per share. When eBay acquired PayPal three years later for a staggering $1.5 billion, Thiel's shares translated into an eye-popping return of $55.5 million, a testament to the transformative power of strategic investing within a Roth IRA.

But Thiel's success did not end there. Buoyed by the windfall from the PayPal acquisition, Thiel reinvested his profits into another startup, Facebook. A $500,000 investment in the social media giant ballooned into approximately $1 billion, and today stands at an estimated $5 billion, all neatly tucked away in his tax-free Roth IRA. The magnitude of Thiel's tax-free gains underscores the importance of holding investments like these within a Roth setup—where taxes are paid up-front rather than on withdrawals later down the line when values could have increased significantly.

To grasp how someone might amass a Mega IRA worth more than $5 million, we must first understand the basic math behind reaching such lofty heights. The annual contribution limits for IRAs, while generous, pale in comparison to the astronomical sums accumulated by Thiel and his ilk. Even maxing out contributions for three decades straight may not be enough to achieve Mega IRA status, especially given the limitations of investment returns and the realities of fluctuating market conditions.

Yet, as we shall discover, the strategies employed by insiders and elites offer a path to circumvent these obstacles and achieve extraordinary levels of wealth within retirement accounts. Investing in non-publicly traded shares and partnership interests emerges as a key strategy for turbocharging IRA growth, offering access to exclusive investment opportunities and exponential returns unattainable through traditional investment vehicles.

The domain of private equity presents another avenue for building Mega IRAs, with unique share classes and carried interest offering the potential for outsized returns. By strategically positioning themselves within private equity firms, individuals can leverage their insider status to emulate Thiel's Roth IRA approach and multiply their retirement savings many times over.

But what about those who lack access to private equity or exclusive investment opportunities? For them, alternative investment platforms like Equifund offer a lifeline, providing access to early-stage investments in promising companies that could deliver above-market returns. While the risks are higher and the path to wealth may be less certain, the potential rewards are undeniable for those willing to take the plunge.

As we navigate the intricacies of Mega IRAs and the strategies employed to build them, it is essential to consider the policy landscape surrounding these accounts. The Senate Finance Committee's concerns over tax revenue loss and potential policy changes loom large, prompting questions about the ethical implications of exploiting tax loopholes for personal gain. While Mega IRAs may offer a path to wealth for some, they also raise thorny questions about fairness, equity, and the distribution of wealth in society.

In "How To Grow A 5 Billion Dollar IRA," we confront these questions head-on, offering a comprehensive guide for readers seeking to understand, emulate, or critique the strategies employed by the financial elite to build extraordinary wealth within their retirement accounts. Through a blend of education, analysis, and introspection, readers are empowered to make informed decisions about their own financial futures and contribute to a more equitable and transparent financial system.

It is important to note that the purpose of this book is not to cast judgment on Peter Thiel or portray him as a "bad" person. The information presented in this book is based on publicly available facts and serves to analyze the strategies and tactics employed by Thiel and other financial elites to build Mega IRAs. While some may question the ethics or fairness of certain wealth-building techniques, it is acknowledged that Thiel appears to have operated within the bounds of the law. The intention of this book is to provide readers with a deeper understanding of the complexities of wealth accumulation within retirement accounts, help them achieve their goals, and to spark discussions about the broader implications for society.

Join me as we unlock the secrets of Mega IRAs and explore the possibilities and perils of growing a $5 billion retirement account. The road ahead is fraught with challenges and uncertainties, but for those willing to seize the opportunity, the rewards may be beyond their wildest dreams. Welcome to the world of Mega IRAs, where the stakes are high, the strategies are bold, and the wealth knows no bounds.

Chapter 1: The Evolution of the IRA

The Birth of the IRA: A Brief History

The concept of retirement savings has undergone a remarkable evolution throughout history, with the modern Individual Retirement Account (IRA) emerging as a cornerstone of financial planning for millions of Americans. The roots of the IRA can be traced back to the early 20th century, a time when retirement security was far from guaranteed for the average worker. In response to growing concerns about the financial well-being of retirees, policymakers sought to create a vehicle for individuals to save and invest for their golden years.

The precursor to the IRA came in the form of pension plans, which were originally established by employers to provide retirement benefits to their employees. However, these plans were often limited in scope and accessibility, leaving many workers without adequate retirement savings. Recognizing the need for a more inclusive and portable retirement savings option, policymakers introduced the concept of the IRA in the 1970s.

The IRA was officially born with the passage of the Employee Retirement Income Security Act (ERISA) in 1974, which laid the groundwork for the modern retirement savings landscape. The original IRA allowed individuals to contribute a portion of their earnings to a tax-deferred savings account, with contributions being tax-deductible and investment earnings growing tax-free until retirement. This groundbreaking legislation marked a significant step forward in democratizing retirement savings and empowering individuals to take control of their financial futures.

Over the years, the IRA underwent several revisions and expansions to accommodate changing economic realities and evolving retirement needs. The Tax Reform Act of 1986 introduced the Traditional IRA, which allowed individuals to make tax-deductible contributions regardless of whether they were covered by an employer-sponsored retirement plan. This expanded access to retirement savings for millions of Americans and laid the foundation for the widespread adoption of IRAs as a key component of retirement planning.

Understanding Traditional vs. Roth IRAs

As the popularity of IRAs continued to grow, policymakers recognized the need for greater flexibility and choice in retirement savings options. In 1997, the Taxpayer Relief Act introduced the Roth IRA, a new type of retirement account that offered a unique set of benefits and features compared to its traditional counterpart. While both Traditional and Roth

IRAs share the common goal of helping individuals save for retirement, they differ in key aspects such as tax treatment, contribution limits, and withdrawal rules.

The Traditional IRA operates on a tax-deferred basis, meaning that contributions are typically tax-deductible in the year they are made, and investment earnings grow tax-free until retirement. However, withdrawals from a Traditional IRA are subject to income tax at the individual's ordinary income tax rate, potentially leading to a significant tax burden in retirement.

In contrast, the Roth IRA offers tax-free growth and withdrawals, but contributions are made with after-tax dollars and are not tax-deductible. This means that while individuals do not receive an immediate tax benefit for contributing to a Roth IRA, they can enjoy tax-free withdrawals in retirement, including both contributions and earnings. Additionally, Roth IRAs do not have required minimum distributions (RMDs) during the account holder's lifetime, providing greater flexibility and control over retirement income planning.

The choice between a Traditional and Roth IRA depends on individual circumstances such as current tax bracket, expected future tax rates, and retirement goals. While Traditional IRAs may be more advantageous for individuals in higher tax brackets who expect to be in a lower tax bracket in retirement, Roth IRAs offer valuable tax diversification and the potential for tax-free growth in retirement.

The Rise of the Mega IRA: Examining the Phenomenon

Against the backdrop of this evolving retirement savings landscape, a new phenomenon has emerged; the Mega IRA. Defined by its astronomical size and tax-free status, the Mega IRA represents the pinnacle of retirement savings success, with account balances reaching into the billions of dollars. At the forefront of this phenomenon is Peter Thiel, whose legendary Roth IRA has become the stuff of Wall Street lore.

Thiel's Roth IRA success story is a testament to the power of strategic investing and long-term vision. By seizing opportunities to invest in high-growth companies through a tax-advantaged account, Thiel was able to multiply his initial capital many times over and accumulate vast wealth within his Roth IRA. The magnitude of Thiel's tax-free gains underscores the importance of holding investments like these within a Roth setup, where taxes are paid upfront rather than on withdrawals later down the line when values could have increased significantly.

But Thiel is not alone in his pursuit of Mega IRA status. Across industries and sectors, savvy investors and financial elites are leveraging the unique advantages of IRAs to build extraordinary levels of wealth within their retirement accounts. From early-stage startups to private equity investments, the strategies employed by these individuals offer valuable insights into the potential of retirement savings as a vehicle for wealth accumulation.

A Brief History of the 401(k)

The 401(k) retirement savings plan has become a cornerstone of retirement planning for millions of Americans since its inception in the late 1970s. The origins of the 401(k) can be traced back to a provision in the Revenue Act of 1978, which allowed employees to defer compensation from bonuses and stock options into tax-deferred retirement accounts. While initially intended as a tax loophole for executives and highly compensated employees, the 401(k) would soon evolve into a widely accessible retirement savings vehicle for workers across all income levels.

The watershed moment for the 401(k) came in 1980 when the Internal Revenue Service (IRS) issued a ruling that allowed employees to contribute to their retirement accounts through salary deductions, rather than relying solely on employer contributions. This groundbreaking change democratized retirement savings and paved the way for the widespread adoption of the 401(k) as a primary retirement savings vehicle.

Throughout the 1980s and 1990s, the popularity of the 401(k) continued to soar as employers embraced the cost-saving benefits of offering defined contribution plans over traditional defined benefit pensions. Unlike pensions, which guaranteed a set retirement income based on years of service and salary, 401(k) plans shifted the responsibility for retirement savings from employers to employees, empowering individuals to take control of their financial futures.

The Tax Reform Act of 1986 further bolstered the appeal of 401(k) plans by allowing employees to make tax-deductible contributions to their accounts, up to specified limits set by the IRS. Additionally, the Act introduced the concept of employer matching contributions, whereby employers would match a portion of employees' contributions to their retirement accounts, effectively doubling their savings.

In the decades that followed, the 401(k) became the predominant retirement savings vehicle in the United States, with millions of workers relying on these accounts to build wealth for retirement. Despite criticisms of high fees, limited investment options, and inadequate savings rates, the 401(k) remains a vital tool for retirement planning and wealth accumulation.

Today, the 401(k) landscape continues to evolve, with policymakers and employers exploring ways to enhance retirement savings options and improve retirement outcomes for workers. From automatic enrollment and escalation features to the introduction of target-date funds and low-cost index funds, efforts are underway to make 401(k) plans more accessible, affordable, and effective for all Americans.

It's clear that this retirement savings plan has had a profound impact on the financial lives of millions of individuals and families. From its humble beginnings as a tax loophole for executives to its status as a ubiquitous retirement savings vehicle, the 401(k) represents a testament to the power of innovation, ingenuity, and collective action in shaping the future of retirement security in America.

As we continue our exploration of Mega IRAs in the chapters ahead, we will go deeper into the strategies and tactics employed by the financial elite to achieve unimaginable levels of wealth within their retirement accounts. From understanding contribution limits to maximizing investment returns, readers will gain practical insights and actionable strategies for building their own path to retirement success. Join us as we unravel the secrets of Mega IRAs and unlock the potential of tax-advantaged investing for a secure financial future.

Chapter 2: The Peter Thiel Strategy

Decoding Peter Thiel's Roth IRA Success Story

Peter Thiel's Roth IRA success story has captivated the financial world, serving as a shining example of the potential for tax-advantaged investing to generate extraordinary wealth. At the core of Thiel's strategy lies a combination of foresight, strategic investing, and a keen understanding of the power of compounding. By harnessing the unique advantages of the Roth IRA, Thiel was able to turn a modest initial investment into billions of dollars in tax-free wealth. In this chapter, we delve into the specifics of Thiel's Roth IRA strategy, uncovering the secrets behind his unprecedented success and exploring the lessons that can be learned from his journey.

Investing in High-Growth Companies: PayPal to Facebook

Thiel's journey to Mega IRA status began with a series of strategic investments in high-growth companies, starting with his early involvement in PayPal. In 1999, Thiel made a modest investment of just $1,700 to acquire 1.7 million shares of PayPal at a par value of $0.001 per share. This seemingly inconsequential investment would prove to be the catalyst for Thiel's meteoric rise to wealth within his Roth IRA.

Three years later, eBay acquired PayPal for a staggering $1.5 billion, catapulting Thiel's investment to new heights and generating a return of $55.5 million, an astonishing feat by any measure. The success of the PayPal investment served as validation of Thiel's investment thesis and laid the groundwork for future ventures in the world of high-growth technology companies.

Buoyed by the windfall from the PayPal acquisition, Thiel set his sights on the next frontier of technological innovation; social media. In 2004, he made a strategic investment of $500,000 in a then-little-known company named Facebook, which was founded by Mark Zuckerberg and his college roommates. Thiel's investment in Facebook would prove to be one of the most lucrative decisions of his career, ultimately ballooning to approximately $1 billion and solidifying his status as a visionary investor.

The success of Thiel's investments in PayPal and Facebook underscores the transformative power of strategic investing in high-growth companies. By identifying and capitalizing on emerging trends and disruptive technologies, Thiel was able to generate outsized returns and multiply his initial capital many times over. Moreover, by holding these investments within a tax-advantaged Roth IRA, Thiel was able to enjoy tax-free growth and withdrawals, maximizing the impact of his investment gains.

Lessons Learned: The Power of Tax-Advantaged Investing

Thiel's Roth IRA success story offers valuable lessons for investors seeking to emulate his achievements and build wealth within their retirement accounts. At the heart of Thiel's strategy is a deep appreciation for the unique advantages of tax-advantaged investing, particularly within a Roth IRA. By paying taxes upfront on contributions and enjoying tax-free growth and withdrawals in retirement, investors can unlock the full potential of their investments and minimize their tax burden over time.

One key takeaway from Thiel's story is the importance of long-term vision and patience in investing. While Thiel's investments in PayPal and Facebook may have seemed risky or unconventional at the time, his foresight and conviction ultimately paid off handsomely. By staying true to his investment thesis and resisting the temptation to succumb to short-term market fluctuations, Thiel was able to ride out volatility and capitalize on the exponential growth potential of his investments.

Additionally, Thiel's success underscores the importance of strategic diversification and portfolio management in retirement savings. While Thiel's investments in PayPal and Facebook were undeniably lucrative, they were also high-risk and concentrated in a few select companies. For the average investor, such concentrated bets may not be advisable, and diversification across asset classes and sectors can help mitigate risk and optimize returns over the long term.

Ultimately, Thiel's Roth IRA success story serves as a beacon of inspiration for investors seeking to build wealth within their retirement accounts. By understanding the power of tax-advantaged investing, identifying high-growth opportunities, and maintaining a long-term perspective, investors can follow in Thiel's footsteps and unlock the full potential of their retirement savings. As we continue our exploration of Mega IRAs in the chapters ahead, we will further dissect Thiel's strategy and uncover additional insights into the world of tax-advantaged investing for wealth accumulation. Join us as we unravel the secrets of Mega IRAs and uncover the keys to financial success in retirement.

Chapter 3: Achieving Mega IRA Status

Crunching the Numbers: Understanding Contribution Limits and Investment Returns

Achieving Mega IRA status requires a deep understanding of the numbers involved; contribution limits, investment returns, and the power of compounding. At the heart of this endeavor is the need to maximize contributions while generating robust investment returns over time. Let's break down the key components of Mega IRA accumulation and explore the mathematics behind this ambitious goal.

First and foremost, it's essential to grasp the contribution limits imposed by the IRS on retirement accounts. For 2024, individuals can contribute up to $23,000 to their 401(k) plans, with an additional catch-up contribution of $7,500 for those aged 50 and older. Similarly, the annual contribution limit for IRAs stands at $7,000, with an additional catch-up contribution of $1,000 for individuals aged 50 and older. These limits represent the maximum amount that individuals can contribute to their retirement accounts in a given tax year, serving as the foundation for Mega IRA accumulation.

In addition to contribution limits, investors must also consider the role of investment returns in growing their retirement savings. While traditional investment vehicles like stocks and bonds offer potential for growth, achieving Mega IRA status often requires returns that exceed the average market performance. This means seeking out high-growth opportunities, such as early-stage startups or private equity investments, that have the potential to deliver outsized returns over time.

Understanding the mathematics of compound growth is crucial for investors aiming to achieve Mega IRA status. Compound interest, often referred to as the "eighth wonder of the world," refers to the phenomenon whereby investment returns are reinvested to generate additional returns, leading to exponential growth over time. By harnessing the power of compound interest, investors can amplify the impact of their contributions and accelerate the growth of their retirement savings.

Strategies for Maxing Out Contributions: Challenges and Opportunities

Maxing out contributions to retirement accounts is a cornerstone of achieving Mega IRA status, but it's not without its challenges. For many individuals, reaching the annual contribution limits may seem daunting, especially in the face of competing financial priorities such as debt repayment or saving for other goals. However, with careful planning and disciplined saving habits, it's possible to overcome these challenges and maximize contributions to retirement accounts.

One strategy for maximizing contributions is to automate savings through payroll deductions or automatic transfers from a bank account. By setting up recurring contributions to retirement accounts, individuals can ensure that a portion of their income is allocated towards retirement savings each month, reducing the temptation to spend money on discretionary expenses.

Another strategy is to take advantage of employer-sponsored retirement plans, such as 401(k) plans or 403(b) plans, which often offer matching contributions from employers. By contributing enough to receive the full employer match, individuals can effectively double their contributions and accelerate the growth of their retirement savings. Additionally, employer-sponsored plans may offer higher contribution limits than traditional IRAs, providing an opportunity to turbocharge retirement savings.

For individuals who have maxed out their contributions to employer-sponsored plans, other tax-advantaged savings vehicles such as Health Savings Accounts (HSAs) or 529 college savings plans may offer additional opportunities to save for retirement. By taking advantage of these accounts' tax benefits and flexible withdrawal options, individuals can further diversify their retirement savings and maximize their tax efficiency.

Realizing the Dream: From $1 Million to $5 Billion in Retirement Savings

The path to Mega IRA status may seem daunting, but it's not beyond reach for those willing to put in the effort and discipline required to achieve this ambitious goal. By understanding the contribution limits, harnessing the power of compound growth, and implementing strategies to maximize contributions, individuals can set themselves on a trajectory towards retirement success.

Realizing the dream of a Mega IRA—from $1 million to $5 billion in retirement savings—requires patience, discipline, and a long-term perspective. While the journey may be challenging at times, the rewards are immense for those who persevere. By staying focused on their financial goals and taking proactive steps to grow their retirement savings, individuals can turn their dreams of financial independence into reality.

As we continue our exploration of Mega IRAs in the chapters ahead, we will further dissect the strategies and tactics employed by individuals to achieve extraordinary levels of wealth within their retirement accounts. From understanding investment vehicles to navigating the complexities of tax planning, readers will gain practical insights and actionable strategies for building their own path to retirement success. Join us as we unravel the secrets of Mega IRAs and uncover the keys to financial freedom in retirement.

Chapter 4: Investing in Non-Publicly Traded Shares

Gaining Access to Exclusive Investment Opportunities

Investing in non-publicly traded shares offers a unique opportunity to gain access to exclusive investment opportunities that are not available to the general public. Unlike publicly traded stocks, which are bought and sold on stock exchanges like the New York Stock Exchange (NYSE) or the Nasdaq, non-publicly traded shares are typically offered through private placements, venture capital funds, or direct investments in private companies.

One of the primary advantages of investing in non-publicly traded shares is the potential for outsized returns. Private companies often

experience rapid growth and innovation, outpacing the average market performance and delivering substantial returns to early investors. By gaining access to these high-growth opportunities before they become widely available to the public, investors can position themselves for significant wealth accumulation over time.

However, gaining access to exclusive investment opportunities is not without its challenges. Private investments are often restricted to accredited investors, who are individuals or entities that meet certain income or net worth requirements set by the Securities and Exchange Commission (SEC). This requirement limits the pool of potential investors and can make it difficult for ordinary individuals to participate in private offerings.

Additionally, investing in non-publicly traded shares carries inherent risks, including the lack of liquidity and transparency associated with private investments. Unlike publicly traded stocks, which can be bought and sold on a daily basis, non-publicly traded shares may be subject to lock-up periods or restrictions on transferability, making it difficult for investors to exit their positions in a timely manner. Furthermore, private companies may not be required to disclose the same level of financial information as public companies, making it challenging for investors to assess the company's financial health and performance.

Despite these challenges, investing in non-publicly traded shares offers the potential for significant rewards for investors who are willing to do their due diligence and take calculated risks. By gaining access to exclusive investment opportunities and participating in the growth of innovative companies, investors can diversify their portfolios, enhance their investment returns, and build long-term wealth.

The Ground Floor Advantage: Capitalizing on Start-Up Investments

One of the most compelling aspects of investing in non-publicly traded shares is the opportunity to capitalize on start-up investments at the ground floor. Start-up companies, often referred to as "early-stage" or "pre-revenue" companies, are in the early stages of development and typically have limited operating history and revenue. While investing in start-ups carries inherent risks, including the possibility of failure, successful investments can yield exponential returns for early investors.

One of the key advantages of investing in start-ups is the potential for rapid growth and innovation. Start-up companies are often founded by entrepreneurs with ambitious visions and disruptive ideas, seeking to revolutionize industries and create new markets. By investing in these early-stage ventures, investors can participate in the growth and success of innovative companies and potentially reap substantial rewards as the company matures and scales.

Moreover, investing in start-ups offers the opportunity to diversify one's investment portfolio and access sectors and industries that may be underrepresented in public markets. From technology and biotech to renewable energy and fintech, start-ups are driving innovation and pushing the boundaries of what's possible in today's economy. By gaining exposure to these emerging trends and disruptive technologies, investors can position themselves for long-term growth and capitalize on the next wave of innovation.

However, investing in start-ups requires careful consideration and due diligence to mitigate risks and maximize returns. Start-up investments are inherently speculative and can be highly volatile, with the potential for significant losses if the company fails to execute its business plan or achieve its growth targets. Therefore, it's essential for investors to conduct thorough research, assess the company's management team and business model, and evaluate the market opportunity before making an investment.

The Patience Game: Timing and Maximizing Returns

Investing in non-publicly traded shares requires patience and a long-term perspective to maximize returns. Unlike publicly traded stocks, which can experience rapid price fluctuations and volatility, private investments may take years to mature and realize their full potential. Therefore, it's essential for investors to adopt a patient approach and resist the temptation to make impulsive decisions based on short-term market movements.

One of the keys to maximizing returns on private investments is timing. Successful investors understand that the best opportunities often take time to materialize and are willing to wait patiently for the right moment to exit their positions. By carefully monitoring market trends, assessing the company's progress, and staying informed about industry developments, investors can identify opportune moments to sell their shares and realize profits.

Moreover, investors can enhance their returns by diversifying their portfolio and spreading their investments across multiple companies and sectors. Diversification helps mitigate risk and reduce exposure to any single investment, increasing the likelihood of achieving positive returns over time. By allocating capital to a diverse range of non-publicly traded shares, investors can build a resilient portfolio that is positioned to weather market fluctuations and capitalize on growth opportunities.

Here is a detailed explanation of the SEC requirements regarding accredited investors and the steps individuals can take to gain access to private investments:

1. Understanding Accredited Investors:
Accredited investors are individuals or entities that meet specific criteria established by the SEC, making them eligible to invest in certain private offerings. The rationale behind accrediting investors is that they are presumed to have the financial sophistication and resources necessary to understand and absorb the risks associated with investing in private securities.

2. Income Requirements:
One way to qualify as an accredited investor is by meeting specific income thresholds established by the SEC. As of 2024, an individual must have had an annual income exceeding $200,000 for the past two years ($300,000 for joint income with a spouse) and a reasonable expectation of reaching the same income level in

the current year to qualify as an accredited investor based on income.

3. Net Worth Requirements:
Alternatively, individuals can qualify as accredited investors by meeting certain net worth requirements. To qualify under this criterion, an individual must have a net worth exceeding $1 million, either individually or jointly with a spouse, excluding the value of their primary residence. This threshold is designed to ensure that accredited investors have a sufficient financial cushion to absorb potential investment losses.

4. Entities as Accredited Investors:
In addition to individuals, certain entities can also qualify as accredited investors under the SEC rules. These entities include banks, insurance companies, registered investment companies, and certain types of trusts and partnerships with assets exceeding $5 million. By allowing entities to qualify as accredited

investors, the SEC aims to ensure that institutional investors with substantial resources can participate in private offerings alongside individual investors.

5. Verification Process:
To participate in private offerings as an accredited investor, individuals may be required to provide documentation or other evidence to verify their accredited status. This may include tax returns, financial statements, or certification letters from a qualified professional, such as a certified public accountant (CPA) or attorney. The verification process helps ensure compliance with SEC regulations and confirms that investors meet the necessary criteria to participate in private offerings.

6. Seeking Opportunities:
Once accredited investor status has been established, individuals can explore opportunities to invest in private offerings. These opportunities may include investments in private

equity funds, venture capital funds, hedge funds, real estate partnerships, and direct investments in private companies. Investors can identify potential opportunities through networking, financial advisors, investment platforms, and specialized investment firms that specialize in private offerings.

7. Due Diligence:
Before making any investments, accredited investors should conduct thorough due diligence to assess the risks and potential rewards associated with each opportunity. This may involve reviewing offering documents, financial statements, business plans, and conducting background checks on the management team and other key stakeholders. By conducting due diligence, investors can make informed investment decisions and mitigate the risks associated with private investments.

8. Diversification:

To mitigate risk and enhance returns, accredited investors should consider diversifying their investments across multiple private offerings and asset classes. Diversification helps spread risk and reduce exposure to any single investment, increasing the likelihood of achieving positive returns over time. By allocating capital to a diverse range of private investments, investors can build a resilient portfolio that is positioned to weather market fluctuations and capitalize on growth opportunities.

By understanding the SEC requirements for accredited investors and following these steps, individuals can gain access to private investments and participate in the growth of innovative companies and emerging trends. While investing in private offerings carries inherent risks, accredited investors who conduct thorough due diligence and diversify their portfolios can enhance their investment returns and build long-term wealth.

Recent SEC Amendments to Accredited Investor Definition:

The Securities and Exchange Commission (SEC) recently amended the definition of "accredited investor" under the Securities Act of 1933 to broaden the categories of individuals and entities eligible to participate in private capital markets. These changes aim to identify institutional and individual investors with the knowledge and expertise necessary to engage in private securities offerings effectively. Effective December 8, 2020, the amendments introduce the following key changes:

1. New Categories for Individuals:

Professional Certifications and Designations: The amendments create a category for individual investors who hold certain professional certifications, designations, and other credentials designated by the SEC as qualifying for accredited investor status. Specifically, individuals holding the Series 7, Series 65, or Series 82 licenses administered by the Financial Industry Regulatory Authority (FINRA) in good standing can qualify as accredited investors.

Knowledgeable Employees: Another category introduced is for individual investors who are knowledgeable employees of certain private funds. To qualify, an individual must meet the definition of a "knowledgeable employee" under Rule 3c–5(a)(4) of the Investment Company Act of 1940, which includes directors, executive officers, and employees involved in the investment activities of the private fund or affiliated management person.

Family Clients of Family Offices: Individuals may also qualify as accredited investors based on their status as family clients of family offices. To qualify, an individual must meet specific criteria outlined in Rule 202(a)(11)(G)–1 under the Investment Advisers Act of 1940 and have their investments directed by a knowledgeable person within the family office.

2. New Categories for Entities:

Investment Advisers: Investment advisers registered with the SEC or a state, as well as exempt reporting advisers, may qualify as accredited investors.

Rural Business Investment Companies: Rural business investment companies, as defined in Section 384A of the Consolidated Farm and Rural Development Act, are eligible as accredited investors.

Limited Liability Companies (LLCs): LLCs with assets exceeding $5 million can qualify as accredited investors, provided they were not formed for the sole purpose of acquiring the securities offered.

Family Offices and Family Clients: Family offices meeting specific criteria, including having assets under management exceeding $5 million, may qualify as accredited investors. Similarly, entities defined as family clients under the Investment Advisers Act of 1940 can also qualify if their investments are directed by a qualifying family office.

Catch-All for Other Entities: Entities not covered by existing accredited investor categories, formed for purposes other than acquiring offered securities, and with investments exceeding $5 million, are eligible.

These amendments aim to diversify the pool of accredited investors and provide greater access to private capital markets. Individuals and entities meeting these new criteria can now participate in private offerings, subject to applicable regulations and requirements. These changes reflect the SEC's commitment to promoting capital formation while maintaining investor protection and market integrity.

In conclusion, investing in non-publicly traded shares offers a compelling opportunity to gain access to exclusive investment opportunities, capitalize on start-up investments, and maximize returns over the long term. While investing in private companies carries inherent risks, successful investors can diversify their portfolios, enhance their investment returns, and build long-term wealth by adopting a patient approach, conducting thorough due diligence, and staying informed about market trends. As we continue our exploration of Mega IRAs in the chapters ahead, we will further dissect the strategies and tactics employed by investors to achieve extraordinary levels of wealth within their retirement accounts through investing in non-publicly traded shares. Let's continue to unravel the secrets of Mega IRAs and uncover the keys to financial success in retirement.

Chapter 5: Building Wealth with Private Equity

Private equity investments have long been heralded as a pathway to building substantial wealth, offering opportunities for outsized returns and strategic portfolio diversification. In this chapter, we will delve into the realm of private equity, exploring its potential, the mechanics of leveraging unique share classes, and the coveted advantage of securing carried interest.

Exploring the Potential of Private Equity Investments

Private equity investments involve investing in privately-held companies that are not listed on public stock exchanges. These investments can take various forms, including venture capital, growth equity, and buyouts. Unlike publicly traded stocks, private equity investments are illiquid and typically require a longer investment horizon.

One of the primary attractions of private equity is the potential for substantial returns. Private companies often experience rapid growth and value creation, providing investors with the opportunity to capture significant upside potential. Moreover, private equity investments offer diversification benefits, as they have low correlation with traditional asset classes such as stocks and bonds.

Leveraging Unique Share Classes for Maximum Returns

A key strategy in private equity investing is leveraging unique share classes to maximize returns. Private companies often issue different classes of shares, each with its own rights and preferences. By strategically allocating capital to specific share classes, investors can enhance their risk-adjusted returns and optimize their investment portfolios.

One common approach is to invest in preferred share classes, which typically offer priority in terms of dividend payments and liquidation preferences. Preferred shares often come with fixed dividend rates and downside protection, making them attractive to investors seeking stable income streams and capital preservation.

Another strategy involves investing in common share classes, which offer greater upside potential but may come with higher risk. Common shares typically represent equity ownership in the company and participate in its growth and profitability. By allocating capital to common share classes, investors can capture the full upside potential of successful private companies.

Securing Carried Interest: The Insider Advantage

One of the most coveted advantages of private equity investing is the opportunity to secure carried interest, also known as "carry." Carried interest represents a share of the profits earned by the general partner of a private equity fund, typically calculated as a percentage of the fund's total returns.

Carried interest is often structured as an incentive fee, aligning the interests of the general partner with those of the limited partners (investors) in the fund. General partners typically receive carried interest once certain performance hurdles, known as the "hurdle rate," are met. This incentivizes general partners to generate superior investment returns and maximize the value of the fund's portfolio.

Securing carried interest can be highly lucrative for general partners, providing them with a significant financial incentive to drive value creation and outperform the market. However, it is important to note that carried interest is typically subject to a "clawback" provision, which allows limited partners to reclaim a portion of the carried interest if certain conditions are not met.

Private equity encompasses a wide range of investment strategies and opportunities. Here are some examples of private equity investment types:

Venture Capital: Venture capital firms invest in early-stage and high-growth companies with the potential for significant returns. These investments typically focus on technology, healthcare, and other innovative industries.

Examples of venture capital-backed companies include:
Uber: A ride-hailing company that revolutionized the transportation industry.
Airbnb: A platform that allows individuals to rent out their homes or properties to travelers.

SpaceX: A private aerospace manufacturer and space transportation company founded by Elon Musk.

Buyouts: Buyout firms acquire established companies with the goal of improving operations, increasing profitability, and ultimately selling the company for a profit. Buyout transactions can take various forms, including leveraged buyouts (LBOs) and management buyouts (MBOs).

Examples of companies acquired through buyouts include:
Heinz: The food processing company was acquired by Berkshire Hathaway and 3G Capital in a $28 billion leveraged buyout.
Dell Technologies: The computer technology company was taken private by Silver Lake Partners and Michael Dell in a $24 billion buyout.
Toys "R" Us: The toy retailer was acquired by Bain Capital, KKR & Co., and Vornado Realty Trust in a leveraged buyout.

Private Debt: Private equity firms may also invest in debt securities issued by private companies. These investments can take the form of senior secured loans, mezzanine debt, or distressed debt.

Examples of private debt investments include:
Loans provided to finance leveraged buyouts or recapitalizations of private companies.
Mezzanine financing to support growth initiatives or acquisitions.
Distressed debt investments in companies facing financial challenges or undergoing restructuring.

Growth Equity: Growth equity firms invest in established companies that are experiencing rapid growth but may not yet be profitable. These investments are often used to support expansion initiatives, product development, or market expansion.

Examples of growth equity investments include:

Peloton: The fitness technology company received growth equity financing to support its expansion into new markets and product development efforts.

Stripe: The online payment processing company raised growth equity funding to fuel its international expansion and product innovation.

Robinhood: The financial services company secured growth equity financing to support its platform expansion and product diversification efforts.

These examples illustrate the diverse range of investment opportunities within the private equity asset class, spanning from early-stage startups to established companies undergoing transformation or growth.

Investing in private equity can be a lucrative venture, but it requires careful consideration and a strategic approach. Here's a detailed step-by-step guide for readers interested in investing in private equity:

Step 1: Educate Yourself

Before diving into private equity investing, take the time to educate yourself about the asset class. Familiarize yourself with the different types of private equity investments, such as venture capital, growth equity, and buyouts. Understand the risks and rewards associated with each type of investment, as well as the mechanics of private equity fund structures.

Step 2: Assess Your Investment Goals and Risk Tolerance

Consider your investment goals, time horizon, and risk tolerance. Private equity investments are typically illiquid and require a long-term commitment, so make sure your investment horizon aligns with the illiquidity of private equity funds. Additionally, assess your risk tolerance and determine how much of your portfolio you're comfortable allocating to private equity.

Step 3: Determine Your Investment Strategy

Develop a clear investment strategy based on your goals and risk tolerance. Decide whether you want to invest directly in individual private companies or through private equity funds. Direct investments offer more control and potentially higher returns but require substantial expertise and due diligence. Private equity funds provide diversification and professional management but may have higher fees and less transparency.

Step 4: Identify Investment Opportunities

Once you've defined your investment strategy, start looking for investment opportunities. Network with industry professionals, attend conferences and events, and consider joining angel investor groups or venture capital networks. You can also explore online platforms that connect investors with private companies seeking funding.

Step 5: Perform Due Diligence

Before making any investments, conduct thorough due diligence on potential opportunities. Evaluate the company's business model, market potential, competitive landscape, management team, and financial performance. Review legal documents, such as offering memoranda and investment agreements, and seek advice from legal and financial professionals.

Step 6: Structure Your Investment

Once you've identified a promising investment opportunity, structure your investment accordingly. If investing directly, negotiate terms with the company and draft a comprehensive investment agreement. If investing through a private equity fund, review the fund's offering documents and complete the necessary subscription paperwork.

Step 7: Monitor Your Investments

After making your investment, stay actively involved in monitoring its performance. Keep abreast of company developments, industry trends, and market conditions that may impact your investment. Communicate regularly with the company's management team or the fund's general partner to track progress and address any concerns.

Step 8: Manage Your Portfolio

As you build your private equity portfolio, maintain a balanced allocation across different investments and asset classes. Diversify your portfolio to spread risk and maximize returns. Consider periodically rebalancing your portfolio to adjust for changes in market conditions or your investment objectives.

Step 9: Stay Informed and Adapt

Continue to educate yourself about developments in the private equity market and adapt your investment strategy accordingly. Stay informed about regulatory changes, economic trends, and emerging opportunities in the private equity landscape. Be prepared to adjust your portfolio as needed to optimize performance and mitigate risks.

Step 10: Seek Professional Advice

Consider seeking advice from qualified professionals, such as financial advisors, attorneys, and accountants, who specialize in private equity investing. They can provide valuable insights and guidance to help you navigate the complexities of the private equity market and make informed investment decisions.

By following these steps and exercising diligence and patience, readers can embark on a successful journey into the world of private equity investing and potentially unlock significant wealth-building opportunities.

In summary, private equity investments offer compelling opportunities for building wealth and achieving financial success. By exploring the potential of private equity, leveraging unique share classes, and securing carried interest, investors can unlock the full potential of this dynamic asset class and position themselves for long-term prosperity.

Chapter 6: The Policy Landscape: Senate Finance Committee Response

In recent years, the exponential growth of Mega IRAs, exemplified by cases such as Peter Thiel's, has raised significant concerns among policymakers regarding tax revenue loss and its implications for economic disparity. This chapter explores the response of the Senate Finance Committee to these concerns, potential policy changes to address tax avoidance, and the delicate balance between tax benefits and wealth distribution.

Concerns Over Mega IRAs: Loss of Tax Revenue and Policy Implications

The Senate Finance Committee has expressed growing concern over the proliferation of Mega

IRAs and the potential loss of tax revenue associated with these accounts. Mega IRAs, which amass billions of dollars in tax-free gains, raise questions about the fairness of the tax system and the distribution of benefits. Policymakers worry that high-income individuals may exploit Roth IRA tax benefits to avoid paying their fair share of taxes, exacerbating economic inequality and widening the wealth gap.

The case of Peter Thiel, who accumulated a $5 billion tax-free gain in his Roth IRA, epitomizes the concerns surrounding Mega IRAs. While Thiel's investment strategy was legal and within the bounds of existing tax laws, the sheer magnitude of his tax-free gains has prompted calls for closer scrutiny and potential policy reforms.

Potential Policy Changes: Addressing Tax Avoidance and Economic Disparity

In response to concerns over Mega IRAs, the Senate Finance Committee is considering potential policy changes to address tax avoidance and mitigate economic disparity. These policy changes could take various forms, including amendments to contribution limits, qualification requirements, and tax benefits related to Roth IRAs.

One proposed policy change is to cap contributions to Roth IRAs at a certain level, such as $5 million, to prevent individuals from accumulating excessively large tax-free gains. This would ensure that Roth IRAs continue to serve their intended purpose of helping middle-class families save for retirement without providing excessive tax benefits to high-income individuals.

Another proposed change is to mandate account holders to take out sizable funds from their Mega IRAs to prevent indefinite accumulation of tax-free gains. By imposing minimum distribution requirements, policymakers can ensure that Mega IRAs contribute to tax revenue generation and prevent individuals from using these accounts solely for tax avoidance purposes.

Additionally, policymakers may explore reforms to qualification requirements for Roth IRAs to ensure that these accounts are accessible to middle-class families while preventing abuse by high-income individuals. This could involve tightening income eligibility criteria or imposing stricter limits on the types of investments allowed within Roth IRAs.

Navigating the Future: Balancing Tax Benefits and Wealth Distribution

As policymakers navigate the future of retirement savings and tax policy, striking a balance between providing tax benefits for retirement savings and promoting equitable wealth distribution remains paramount. While

Roth IRAs offer valuable tax advantages for middle-class families, policymakers must ensure that these benefits are not exploited by high-income individuals to the detriment of tax revenue and economic equality.

Moreover, any policy changes aimed at addressing Mega IRAs must be carefully crafted to avoid unintended consequences and ensure that retirement savings incentives remain effective. Balancing the need for tax revenue generation with the goal of promoting retirement security and financial stability for all Americans requires thoughtful consideration and collaboration across political divides.

In conclusion, the response of the Senate Finance Committee to concerns over Mega IRAs underscores the importance of addressing tax avoidance and economic disparity through targeted policy reforms. By enacting prudent changes to Roth IRA rules and qualification requirements, policymakers can safeguard the integrity of the tax system and promote a more equitable distribution of wealth. However, achieving this balance will require careful deliberation and bipartisan cooperation to ensure that retirement savings incentives remain fair and effective for all Americans.

Chapter 7: Final Considerations and Cautionary Tales

As we conclude our exploration of Mega IRAs and the intricacies of tax-advantaged retirement savings, it's crucial to reflect on the temptations, risks, and ethical considerations associated with these accounts. In this final chapter, we delve into the allure of Mega IRAs, the importance of financial literacy and professional guidance, and the broader ethical implications of retirement savings and wealth accumulation.

The Temptation of Mega IRAs: Balancing Risk and Reward

Mega IRAs represent the pinnacle of tax-advantaged retirement savings, offering the potential for astronomical gains without the burden of taxation. However, the allure of Mega

IRAs comes with inherent risks and ethical considerations. While individuals may be tempted to pursue aggressive investment strategies and exploit tax loopholes to maximize their gains, it's essential to balance the pursuit of wealth with prudent risk management and long-term financial planning.

The case of Peter Thiel serves as both an inspiration and a cautionary tale. Thiel's astute investment decisions and strategic use of Roth IRAs catapulted him to billionaire status, showcasing the power of tax-advantaged investing. However, the extraordinary size of Thiel's Mega IRA raises questions about fairness, equity, and the integrity of the tax system. As individuals navigate the complexities of retirement savings, they must weigh the potential rewards of tax-advantaged investing against the ethical implications of extreme wealth accumulation.

The Importance of Financial Literacy and Professional Guidance

Amidst the complexities of retirement planning and tax optimization, the importance of financial literacy and professional guidance cannot be overstated. Many individuals lack the knowledge and expertise to navigate the nuances of tax-advantaged retirement accounts effectively. Without proper education and guidance, they may fall prey to risky investment strategies, tax avoidance schemes, or unethical practices.

Financial literacy empowers individuals to make informed decisions about their retirement savings, understand the implications of tax strategies, and plan for long-term financial security. By educating themselves about retirement planning principles, investment fundamentals, and tax laws, individuals can make sound choices that align with their goals and values.

Moreover, seeking guidance from qualified professionals, such as financial advisors, tax experts, and legal counsel, can provide invaluable insights and peace of mind. These professionals can offer personalized advice, recommend suitable investment strategies, and help individuals navigate the complexities of retirement planning in a responsible and ethical manner.

Ensuring Retirement Security for All: Ethical Considerations and Social Responsibility

As we contemplate the future of retirement savings and wealth accumulation, it's imperative to consider the broader ethical implications and social responsibilities associated with financial success. While tax-advantaged retirement accounts offer valuable benefits for individuals seeking to secure their financial futures, they also raise questions about economic inequality, social justice, and the common good.

In a society marked by widening wealth disparities and systemic inequities, ensuring retirement security for all Americans requires a collective commitment to fairness, inclusivity, and social responsibility. Policymakers, financial institutions, and individuals alike must strive to create an equitable and sustainable retirement system that prioritizes the needs of all citizens, regardless of their wealth or privilege.

Ethical considerations should guide our approach to retirement planning and tax optimization, encouraging individuals to act with integrity, transparency, and social consciousness. By embracing ethical principles and prioritizing the well-being of others, we can build a retirement system that fosters prosperity, equality, and shared prosperity for generations to come.

In conclusion, Mega IRAs offer tantalizing opportunities for tax-advantaged retirement savings, but they also pose ethical dilemmas and risks. By balancing the pursuit of wealth with responsible financial stewardship, fostering financial literacy and seeking professional guidance, and embracing ethical considerations and social responsibility, individuals can navigate the complexities of retirement planning with integrity and purpose. As we strive to ensure retirement security for all Americans, let us approach the future with wisdom, compassion, and a commitment to the common good.

Conclusion

Retirement planning stands as one of the most complex and critical endeavors individuals undertake in their lifetime. As we conclude our exploration of retirement planning, tax-advantaged investment strategies, and the quest for financial security, it's essential to reflect on the multifaceted nature of this journey, empower individuals with knowledge and guidance, and envision a future that promotes equity, prosperity, and well-being for all.

Reflecting on the Complexity of Retirement Planning

Retirement planning is a dynamic process that involves much more than simply saving for the future. It requires individuals to navigate a myriad of factors, including investment choices, tax implications, retirement goals, and economic uncertainties. From choosing between traditional and Roth IRAs to optimizing investment returns and managing risk, the complexity of retirement planning underscores the need for careful consideration and informed decision-making.

Empowering Individuals to Navigate the Terrain of Wealth Accumulation

Empowering you to navigate the terrain of wealth accumulation begins with financial literacy and education. By understanding the fundamentals of retirement planning, investment strategies, and tax policy, you can make informed choices that align with their goals and values. Moreover, seeking professional financial advice and guidance can provide invaluable insights, personalized recommendations, and peace of mind.

Looking Ahead: Building a More Equitable Financial Future

As we look ahead to the future of retirement planning and financial security, it's crucial to envision a more equitable and inclusive financial landscape. This requires addressing systemic inequities, promoting social responsibility, and advocating for policies that prioritize the needs of all citizens. By fostering economic empowerment, reducing barriers to financial access, and promoting financial literacy, we can build a future where everyone has the opportunity to achieve their financial goals and live with dignity and purpose.

Additional Information on Retirement Planning, Investment Strategies, and Tax Policy

For individuals seeking to deepen their understanding of retirement planning, investment strategies, and tax policy, there are numerous resources available. From books and online courses to financial planning seminars and workshops, you can access a wealth of information to enhance their knowledge and skills. Additionally, staying informed about changes in tax laws, investment trends, and economic developments is essential for making informed decisions about retirement planning and wealth accumulation.

Recommendations for Seeking Professional Financial Advice and Guidance

While individuals can empower themselves with knowledge and information, seeking professional financial advice and guidance is often invaluable. Financial advisors, tax professionals, and investment experts can offer personalized recommendations, tailored strategies, and objective insights that align with individual goals and circumstances. When selecting a financial advisor, it's essential to consider factors such as experience, credentials, and fiduciary responsibility to ensure that you receive trustworthy and competent advice.

The Myth of Professional Fund Management

Professional fund managers command hefty fees to oversee billions of dollars in assets for investors, leveraging their education and expertise to navigate the complexities of the financial markets. However, the reality often falls short of expectations. Despite their credentials and resources, most professional fund managers struggle to outperform simple, passive investment strategies over the long run.

According to research from S&P Global's SPIVA scorecards, a staggering 92% of active large-cap fund managers have underperformed the S&P 500 index over the last 15 years as of the end of June. This means that the vast majority of actively managed funds fail to beat the performance of a basic index fund tracking the broader market.

Even over shorter time horizons, the track record of active fund managers remains lackluster. Less than 40% of active managers could outperform the S&P 500 over the past year, highlighting the challenges of consistently beating the market.

The Power of Passive Investing

Contrary to popular belief, investors don't need special insights or sophisticated strategies to outperform the majority of professional fund managers. A simple, hands-off approach known as passive investing can often yield superior results over the long term.

By investing in low-cost index funds that track major market benchmarks like the S&P 500, such as the Vanguard S&P 500 ETF (VOO), individuals can achieve broad diversification and market-matching returns without the need for active management or stock-picking prowess. This approach allows investors to capture the overall growth of the market while minimizing fees and reducing the risks associated with trying to outsmart the market.

In essence, the data suggests that the vast majority of investors would be better off embracing passive investing strategies rather than entrusting their hard-earned money to active fund managers who often struggle to deliver on their promises of market-beating returns.

In conclusion, the journey towards financial security and retirement planning is a lifelong endeavor that requires careful planning, informed decision-making, and ongoing vigilance. By reflecting on the complexity of retirement planning, empowering individuals with knowledge and guidance, and envisioning a more equitable financial future, we can create a world where everyone has the opportunity to achieve their financial goals and live with confidence and security.

Harmony Weaver

www.ingramcontent.com/pod-product-compliance
Lightning Source LLC
Chambersburg PA
CBHW070311230526
45470CB00002B/815